Name That
Bible Character
Grades 4-6

by Sharon Thompson

Carson-Dellosa Christian Publishing
Greensboro, North Carolina

Our Mission

It is the mission of Carson-Dellosa Christian Publishing
to create the highest-quality Scripture-based children's products
that teach the Word of God, share His love and goodness,
assist in faith development, and glorify His Son, Jesus Christ.

". . . teach me your ways so I may know you. . . ."
Exodus 33:13

Credits

Project Director: Sherrill B. Flora
Editor: Carol Layton
Inside Illustrations: Vanessa Booth
Cover Illustration: Dan Sharp

Printed in the USA · All rights reserved.   **ISBN 0-88724-225-1**

Table of Contents

From Dust to Dust

Read the clues and the Bible verse to name that Bible character!

1. His grandson's name was Enosh.
2. He had a third son named Seth.
3. This character said, "This is now bone of my bones and flesh of my flesh."
4. He hid from the Lord because he was naked.
5. God created a suitable helper for this man.
6. He and his wife ate fruit from the forbidden tree.
7. Read about this Bible character in **Genesis 2:20.**

_____
Name that Bible character!

Write the letters on the matching animals on the line below to find out who this man is and what was special about him.

_____

She Was Deceived

Read the clues and the Bible verse to name that Bible character!

1. God created her from her husband's rib.
2. She listened to a serpent and disobeyed God.
3. She and her husband caused the fall of man.
4. She hid from the Lord in a garden.
5. One of her sons killed his brother.
6. She had a son named Seth.
7. Read about this Bible character in **Genesis 3:20.**

_____
Name that Bible character!

Cross out the letters S, I, and N one time in each set of letters below to find words that relate to this woman. Find her name in #10.

1. SSIERPENNT _____

2. SEIDENN _____

3. NNASKEID _____

4. SSHAIMNE _____

5. SGIARDENN _____

6. SHIIDINNG _____

7. SCUIRNSE _____

8. CHSIILDRENN _____

9. SWOIMANN _____

10. ESIVNE _____

He Had Faith

Read the clues and the Bible verse to name that Bible character!

1. He was a righteous man.
2. He had three sons: Ham, Shem, and Japheth.
3. God told him about a great flood that was coming to Earth.
4. God told this man precisely how to build an ark.
5. He saved his family and every kind of animal from a flood that covered Earth.
6. God told him about His rainbow covenant.
7. Read about this Bible character in **Genesis 6:9.**

_____
Name that Bible character!

In the hidden picture below find the letters that spell this man's name along with: hammer, saw, anchor, ladder, cooking pot, dove, rainbow, and Ham, Shem, and Japheth.

"God Hears"

Read the clues and the Bible verse to name that Bible character!

1. His name means "God hears."
2. He was born when Abraham was 86 years old.
3. This man was the firstborn son of Abraham.
4. He and his mother fled to the desert.
5. God promised Abraham that He would bless this son, although He would not make His covenant with him.
6. His mother's name was Hagar.
7. Read about this Bible character in **Genesis 16:15**.

_____
Name that Bible character!

Use the clues to fill in the crossword puzzle below.

Across

2. God told Abram that his firstborn son would be the father of ___ rulers.
4. Hagar was Sarai's _____.
7. Abram and Sarai lived in ___.
8. The angel said that Hagar's son would be a wild ___ of a man.
9. This boy's name is _____.

Down

1. Hagar was an ___.
3. The angel said he would increase Hagar's ___.
5. An ___ of the Lord spoke to Hagar.
6. Hagar began to ___ Sarai.

Saved From Destruction

Read the clues and the Bible verse to name that Bible character!

1. He was Abraham's nephew.
2. He had two daughters.
3. He invited two angels to his house.
4. This man lived in Sodom, a city that was destroyed by burning sulphur.
5. God spared this man and his family.
6. However, his wife looked back and was turned into a pillar of salt.
7. Read about this Bible character in **Genesis 19:1.**

_____
Name that Bible character!

Fill in each blank with a consonant to make words from the clues above. The circled letters spell this man's name.

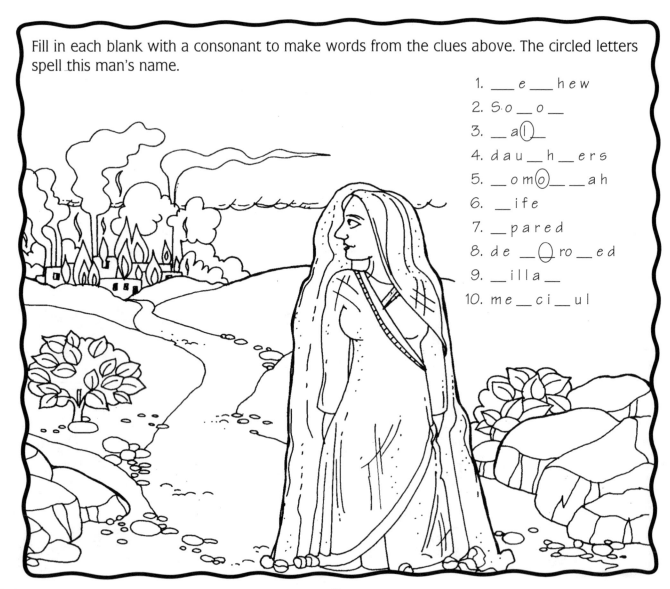

1. ___ e ___ h e w
2. S o ___ o ___
3. ___ a (l)
4. d a u ___ h ___ e r s
5. ___ o m (o) ___ ___ a h
6. ___ i f e
7. ___ p a r e d
8. d e ___ (t) r o ___ e d
9. ___ i l l a ___
10. m e ___ c i ___ u l

8

The Love of His Life

Read the clues and the Bible verse to name that Bible character!

1. She was a shepherdess.
2. This woman's father was Laban.
3. Her sister was Leah.
4. Jacob had to work seven years for her father in order to marry her sister.
5. He had to work another seven years in order to marry this woman.
6. She had two sons named Joseph and Benjamin.
7. Read about this Bible character in **Genesis 29:18.**

_____
Name that Bible character!

Follow the maze from the man to his two wives. Their names are written along the maze route. Circle the letters to name this Bible character.

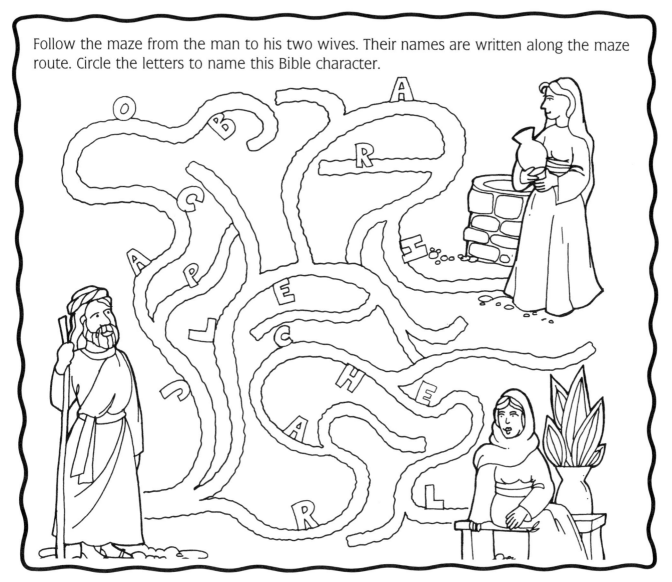

Love Forgives

Read the clues and the Bible verse to name that Bible character!
1. He had 11 brothers.
2. His brothers sold him to merchants.
3. He was in charge of Potiphar's house.
4. Potiphar's wife told her husband that this man tried to attack her.
5. God gave him the ability to interpret dreams.
6. He forgave his brothers and gave them food during the famine.
7. Read about this Bible character in **Genesis 37:2.**

_____
Name that Bible character!

In the picture below, find the letters that spell this man's name along with the following: a cow, 3 sheaves, a vase, 3 stars, a well, and the number 12.

 CD-2046 Name That Bible Character! 4-6

He Led His People

Read the clues and the Bible verse to name that Bible character!

1. His mother hid him to protect him from Pharaoh's order that all baby boys be killed.
2. He killed an Egyptian and buried him in the sand.
3. He ran from Egypt to Midian.
4. God chose him to lead the Israelites out of bondage.
5. He encountered God in a burning bush.
6. He received the Ten Commandments on Mt. Sinai.
7. Read about this Bible character in **Exodus 19:25.**

_____
Name that Bible character!

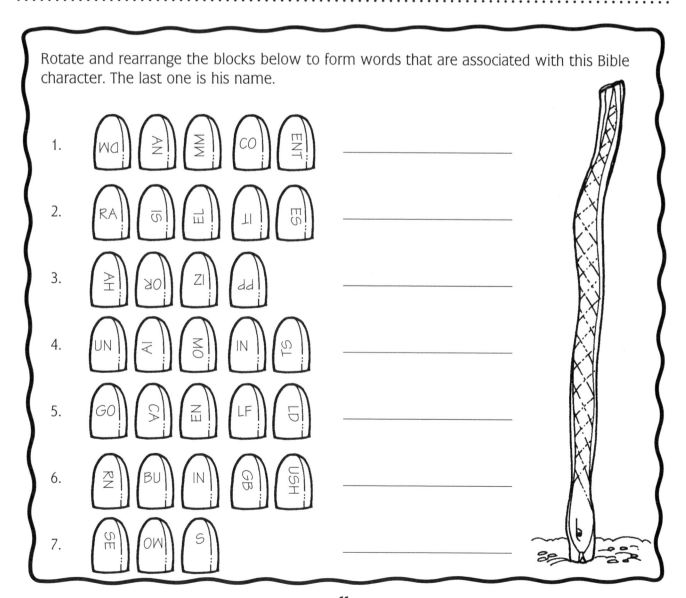

Rotate and rearrange the blocks below to form words that are associated with this Bible character. The last one is his name.

1. DM AN MM CO ENT _____
2. RA IS EL IT ES _____
3. AH OR ZI PP _____
4. UN AI MO IN ST _____
5. GO CA EN LF LD _____
6. RN BU IN GB USH _____
7. SE OW S _____

A Woman of Faith

Read the clues and the Bible verse to name that Bible character!
1. In Hebrews 11, she is called a woman of faith.
2. She hid two Israelite spies in her home.
3. She lived in a house built on the wall of Jericho.
4. Her house was the only one spared when Jericho was destroyed.
5. She was the great-grandmother of King David.
6. She hung a scarlet cord from her window.
7. Read about this Bible character in **Joshua 2:1.**

_____
Name that Bible character!

Unscramble the letters in each circle to identify this woman.

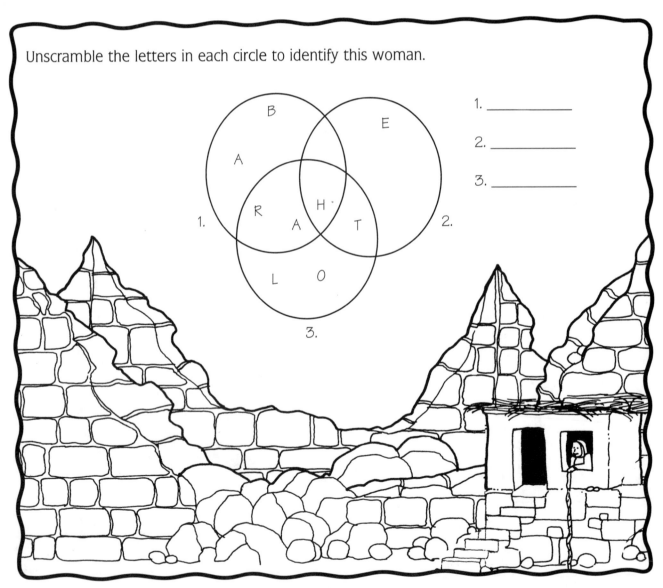

Circle 1: B, A, R, A, H
Circle 2: E, H, T, T
Circle 3: R, A, L, O

1. _____

2. _____

3. _____

CD-2046 Name That Bible Character! 4-6

Love Is Kind

Read the clues and the Bible verse to name that Bible character!

1. This woman was the widow of Elimelech.
2. She and her husband were from Bethlehem.
3. She and her family moved to Moab.
4. Her two sons, Mahlon and Kilion, died.
5. One of her daughters-in-law was named Orpah.
6. Her other daughter-in-law, Ruth, stayed with her to care for her.
7. Read about this Bible character in **Ruth 1:2.**

_____
Name that Bible character!

Use the clues to fill in the crossword puzzle below.

Across

1. another name for Naomi
3. Ruth's first husband's name
5. the city to which Ruth and her mother-in-law returned
8. the name of Ruth and Boaz' son
9. what Ruth gleaned in the fields

Down

2. the name of one of this character's daughters-in-law
4. the name of one of this character's daughters-in-law
6. Boaz became Ruth's ___.
7. the country where Ruth and her mother-in-law were when their husbands died
9. how Ruth got the grain from the field
10. This Bible character's name is ____.

A Man After God's Heart

Read the clues and the Bible verse to name that Bible character!

1. He killed a bear and a lion to protect his sheep.
2. He was a shepherd boy who killed a giant.
3. He played the harp for King Saul.
4. He had a friend named Jonathan.
5. He was chased by Saul but later became king.
6. He wrote many Psalms.
7. Read about this Bible character in the **I Samuel 17:50.**

_____

Name that Bible character!

Use the words provided to fill in the puzzle below.

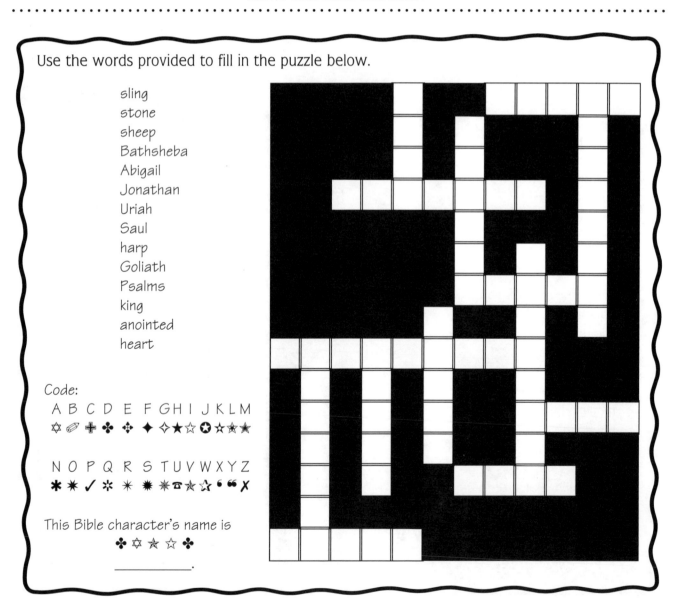

sling
stone
sheep
Bathsheba
Abigail
Jonathan
Uriah
Saul
harp
Goliath
Psalms
king
anointed
heart

Code:

A B C D E F G H I J K L M

N O P Q R S T U V W X Y Z

This Bible character's name is

_____.

A Friend 'til the End

Read the clues and the Bible verse to name that Bible character!
1. This man and his armor bearer killed 20 Philistines within a half an acre of land.
2. He ate honeycomb and was cursed to die by the oath of his father.
3. The people of Israel rescued him so he did not die after eating honey.
4. He and his brothers were killed by Philistines, and his father fell on his sword.
5. His father was King Saul.
6. David was his best friend.
7. Read about this Bible character in **1 Samuel 20:16.**

_____
Name that Bible character!

Cross out the letters S, A, U, and L once in each group of letters below to uncover a word or phrase associated with this Bible character. The last group of letters contains his name.

1. SPHAILISUTINLES _____

2. SAARUMORBLEARER _____

3. STAAMARUISLKTREE _____

4. ISSRAAEULL _____

5. DASAVUILD _____

Saved by the Queen

Read the clues and the Bible verse to name that Bible character!

1. This Jewish man lived during the reign of King Xerxes.
2. This man brought up his cousin because she had neither father nor mother.
3. His cousin was known as Hadassah.
4. He and his cousin helped to save the Jewish people from a wicked decree.
5. Haman hated this man because he wouldn't bow to him.
6. Another name for this man's cousin was Esther.
7. Read about this Bible character in **Esther 2:5.**

_____
Name that Bible character!

Connect the dots to find this man's name.

Dry Bones

Read the clues and the Bible verse to name that Bible character!

1. This man had a vision about the fall of Tyre.
2. God presented a scroll to him and left with the sound of an earthquake.
3. God told this priest to shave his head and cut his beard.
4. God told him to scatter his beard into the wind in every direction.
5. He had a vision of a valley of dry bones.
6. God appeared to this man as a great brightness that lit up the sky.
7. Read about this Bible character in **Ezekiel 1:3.**

_____
Name that Bible character!

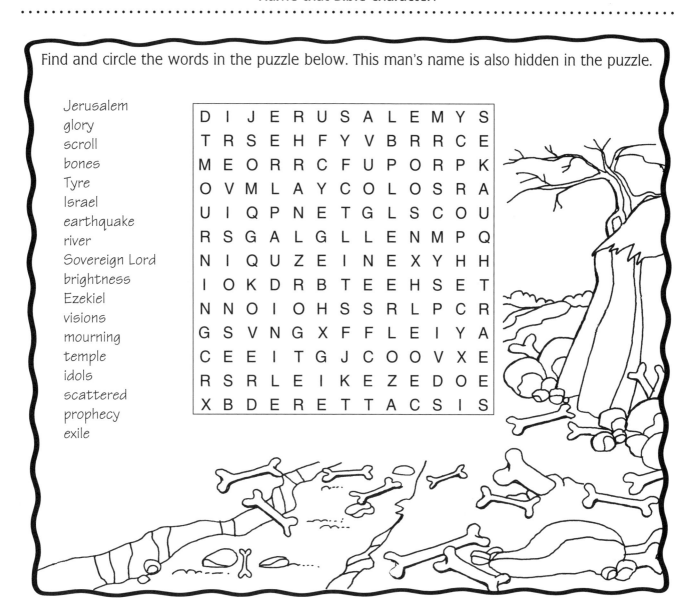

Find and circle the words in the puzzle below. This man's name is also hidden in the puzzle.

Jerusalem
glory
scroll
bones
Tyre
Israel
earthquake
river
Sovereign Lord
brightness
Ezekiel
visions
mourning
temple
idols
scattered
prophecy
exile

```
D I J E R U S A L E M Y S
T R S E H F Y V B R R C E
M E O R R C F U P O R P K
O V M L A Y C O L O S R A
U I Q P N E T G L S C O U
R S G A L G L L E N M P Q
N I Q U Z E I N E X Y H H
I O K D R B T E E H S E T
N N O I O H S S R L P C R
G S V N G X F F L E I Y A
C E E I T G J C O O V X E
R S R L E I K E Z E D O E
X B D E R E T T A C S I S
```

The Man at the Jordan

Read the clues and the Bible verse to name that Bible character!

1. He wore clothes made from camel's hair.
2. He ate locusts and honey.
3. His mother's name was Elizabeth.
4. He was the "voice of one calling in the desert."
5. When he was beheaded, his head was presented to Herodias, Herod's wife.
6. He baptized Jesus and others in the Jordan River.
7. Read about this Bible character in **Mark 1:4.**

_____
Name that Bible character!

Unscramble the letters in each circle to find this Bible character's name.

Circle 1: J O H N T P S A B

1. _____

2. _____

3. _____

Be Born Again!

Read the clues and the Bible verse to name that Bible character!

1. This man accompanied Joseph of Arimathea to Jesus' tomb.
2. He brought myrrh and aloes and wrapped Jesus' body in strips of linen.
3. This man was a Pharisee.
4. He argued with fellow Pharisees that Jesus should not be condemned until he was heard.
5. Jesus told him that no one could see the kingdom of God without being born again.
6. He first met with Jesus at night.
7. Read about this Bible character in **John 3:1**.

_____
Name that Bible character!

Use the clues to fill in the blanks. Then place the numbered letters in the blanks below to spell this man's name.

1. This man belonged to this religious group.

2. The time of day he met Jesus

3. He and Joseph of Arimathea went to the ___.

4. Jesus' body was wrapped in strips of ___.

5. God did not send his son to ___ the world.

6. Whoever lives by the ___ comes into the light.

1.   P __ AR __ SEE __
             1   2

2.   __ I __ __ T
     3

3.   T __ __ B
       4 5

4.   LI __ __ N
          6

5.   __ ON __ EMN
      7   8

6.   TR __ TH
        9

__ __ __ __ __ __ __ __ __
3   1   7   4   8   6   5   9   2

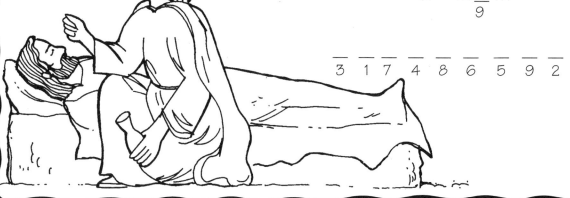

A Loyal Follower

Read the clues and the Bible verse to name that Bible character!

1. Jesus cast seven demons out of this woman.
2. She supported Jesus' ministry.
3. She was present when Jesus died on the cross.
4. She watched Joseph of Arimathea place Jesus' body in the tomb.
5. She went with Jesus' mother and Salome to anoint Jesus' body.
6. Jesus appeared to her after His death.
7. Read about this Bible character in **Luke 8:2**.

_____
Name that Bible character!

Start at the beginning letter and move one square in any direction—up, down, left, right, or diagonally. If you make the right moves, you will spell this Bible character's name.

Start ↓

M	A	A	L	I
S	R	R	A	L
Y	G	D	O	E
M	G	L	N	D
A	D	E	S	E

End ↓

Too Busy to Listen

Read the clues and the Bible verse to name that Bible character!

1. Jesus was a guest in her home.
2. She lived in Bethany with her brother and sister.
3. She complained to Jesus because her sister wouldn't help with housework.
4. Jesus told her that listening to him was better than doing housework.
5. When her brother Lazarus died, Jesus raised him back to life.
6. Jesus loved this woman, her sister, and Lazarus.
7. Read about this Bible character in **Luke 10:41.**

_____
Name that Bible character!

Connect the dots to discover what Jesus said to this Bible character.

Rise Up!

Read the clues and the Bible verse to name that Bible character!

1. This man lived in Bethany.
2. He had two sisters.
3. He became sick and died.
4. His body laid in a tomb for four days.
5. His sisters cried to Jesus about his death.
6. Jesus raised him back to life.
7. Read about this Bible character in **John 11:1**.

_____
Name that Bible character!

Start at the beginning letter and move one square in any direction—up, down, left, right, or diagonally. If you make the right moves, you will spell this man's name.

Start

L	O	Z	L	Y
U	A	L	A	C
Z	R	R	O	F
L	G	L	U	E
U	D	E	S	S

Finish

Lost But Now He's Found

Read the clues and the Bible verse to name that Bible character!

1. This young man asked his father for his share of the estate.
2. He left to live a wild life in a distant country.
3. When famine struck, this man went to work feeding pigs.
4. When he realized the pigs were eating better than he was, he decided to go home.
5. This man's brother was jealous that his father was having a feast for him.
6. His father rejoiced because he had returned.
7. Read about this Bible character in **Luke 15:13.**

_____

Name that Bible character!

Follow the maze to help the son return to his father. The letters that describe this man are hidden on the correct line of the maze. Circle them.

A True Worshiper

Read the clues and the Bible verse to name that Bible character!

1. This woman broke a jar of expensive perfume.
2. She poured the perfume on Jesus' feet.
3. Her brother died and was raised by Jesus.
4. She anointed Jesus for burial.
5. Her sister got angry with her for not helping her serve Jesus.
6. Jesus said that she "had chosen what is better."
7. Read about this Bible character in **John 12:3.**

_____

Name that Bible character!

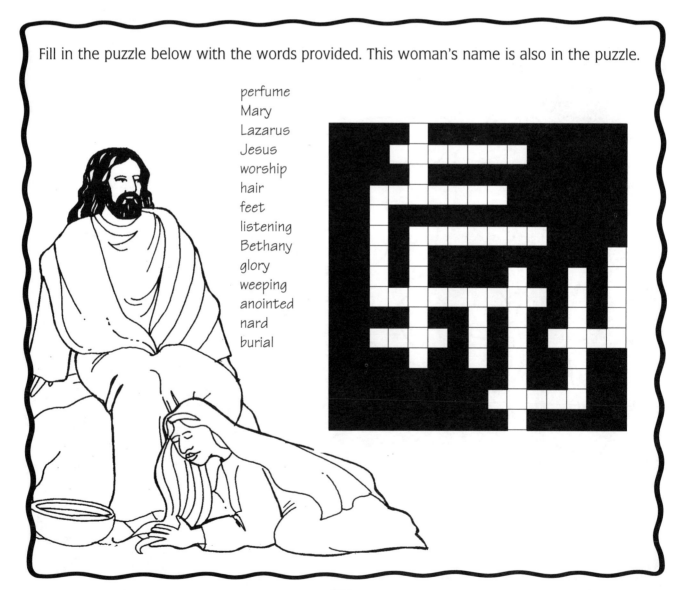

Fill in the puzzle below with the words provided. This woman's name is also in the puzzle.

perfume
Mary
Lazarus
Jesus
worship
hair
feet
listening
Bethany
glory
weeping
anointed
nard
burial

He Sold Out

Read the clues and the Bible verse to name that Bible character!
1. This man was the governor of Judea.
2. He questioned Jesus.
3. His wife told him to have nothing to do with Jesus.
4. He asked the crowd to choose to release either Jesus or Barabbas.
5. He washed his hands of Jesus' blood.
6. He eventually had Jesus flogged and handed him over to be crucified.
7. Read about this Bible character in **Matthew 27:13**.

_____
Name that Bible character!

Rotate and rearrange the crosses below to form words that are associated with this man. The last one is his name.

1. CR FI XI UC ON _____

2. EN OC CE NNI _____

3. BB RA BA AS _____

4. OR NR GO VE _____

5. ER NO SI PR _____

6. TO AE RI PR UM _____

7. HA GO LG OT _____

8. EX UT EC ED _____

9. PI LA TE _____

The Doubter

Read the clues and the Bible verse to name that Bible character!

1. This man was one of the twelve disciples.
2. This disciple was present when Matthias was chosen as the replacement for Judas.
3. This disciple went with Jesus when he raised Lazarus back to life.
4. He was also called Didymus.
5. Jesus told him to stop doubting and believe.
6. Jesus let him touch the nail marks in his hands and the scar on his side.
7. Read about this Bible character in **John 20:24.**

_____
Name that Bible character!

Fill in the puzzle below using the words listed. Two versions of this man's name are also hidden in the puzzle.

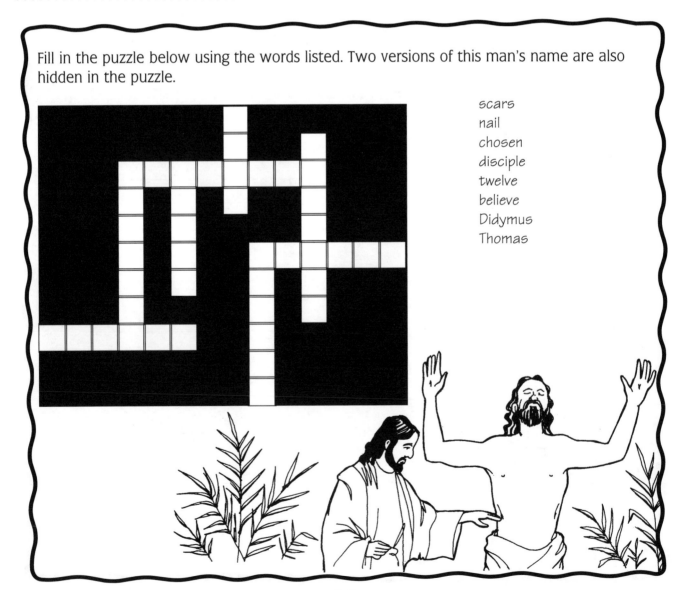

scars
nail
chosen
disciple
twelve
believe
Didymus
Thomas

Dishonesty Doesn't Pay

Read the clues and the Bible verse to name that Bible character!

1. This woman had a husband named Ananias.
2. She and her husband sold their property.
3. She knew that her husband lied about the profits.
4. Her husband died when confronted by Peter about his lie.
5. This woman also lied about how much money they had received.
6. She was buried beside her husband.
7. Read about this Bible character in **Acts 5:1**.

_____

Name that Bible character!

Fill in the blanks. Then arrange the letters in the numbered blanks below to spell this woman's name.

1. Ananias put money at the feet of the ___.
   __ P __ STL__ S
   1

2. This man questioned Ananias about why he lied.
   __ ET __ R
   2

3. Who filled Ananias' heart so that he lied?
   __ AT __ N
   3

4. To whom did he lie?
   __ __ LY   __ P __ R __ T
   4

5. Ananias fell down and ___.
   D __ __ D
   5

6. Ananias' wife showed up about three ___ later.
   H __ __ __ S
   6

Her name was __ __ __ __ __ __ __ __
              3 1 2 2 4 5 6 1

A Rock

Read the clues and the Bible verse to name that Bible character!

1. This disciple walked on water.
2. He cut off the ear of the high priest's servant.
3. He denied Jesus three times before the cock crowed.
4. He wrote two letters to suffering Christians.
5. He saw a sheet of animals lowered from heaven.
6. Jesus said he would build his church on the truth that God had revealed to this disciple.
7. Read about this Bible character in **Acts 10:9.**

_____
Name that Bible character!

Find in the picture below: 2 coins, 3 fish, 2 letters (the kind you mail), a rooster, fish net, ear, bread, basket, sword, and a boat. This man's name is spelled with the following letters of the alphabet: 16, 5, 20, 5, 18. (A = 1)

Good Overcomes Evil

Read the clues and the Bible verse to name that Bible character!

1. This man approved of stoning Stephen.
2. He voiced murderous threats against followers of Jesus.
3. He had a "blinding" conversion experience.
4. He became an apostle.
5. His letters were sent to numerous early churches.
6. He and Silas sang in prison.
7. Read about this Bible character in **Acts 13:9.**

_____
Name that Bible character!

The new name that the Lord gave this man rhymed with his former name. Both names rhyme with ball. This character's name is _____. Start at the arrow that points up on each circle. Follow the direction of the other arrow and skip a letter as you go around each circle to find the names of some of the cities to which this Bible character sent letters to churches.

1. _____

2. _____

3. _____

4. _____

5. _____

An Early Missionary

Read the clues and the Bible verse to name that Bible character!

1. He was a prophet and teacher.
2. He came from the church at Antioch.
3. The Holy Spirit sanctified him and Paul for ministry.
4. He and Paul ministered to the proconsul.
5. His names means "Son of Encouragement."
6. His disagreement with Paul was over John Mark.
7. Read about this Bible character in **Acts 15:36.**

_____
Name that Bible character!

Connect the dots to find this Bible character's name.

CD-2046 Name That Bible Character! 4-6

Answer Key

Page 4 Adam

Adam was the first man.

Page 5 Eve
1. serpent
2. Eden
3. naked
4. shame
5. garden
6. hiding
7. curse
8. children
9. woman
10. Eve

Page 6 Noah

Page 7 Ishmael

Page 8 Lot
1. nephew
2. Sodom
3. salt
4. daughter
5. Gomorrah
6. wife
7. spared
8. destroyed
9. pillar
10. merciful

Page 9 Rachel

Page 10 Joseph

Page 11 Moses
1. commandment
2. Israelites
3. Zipporah
4. Mount Sinai
5. golden calf
6. burning bush
7. Moses

Page 12 Rahab

Rahab the harlot

Page 13 Naomi

Page 14 David

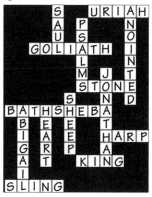

Page 15 Jonathan
1. Philistines
2. armor bearer
3. tamarisk tree
4. Israel
5. David

Page 16 Mordecai

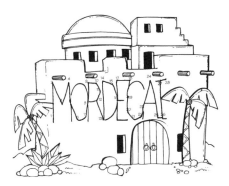

Page 17 Ezekiel

Page 18 John

John the Baptist

Answer Key

Page 19 Nicodemus
1. PHARISEES
2. NIGHT
3. TOMB
4. LINEN
5. CONDEMN
6. TRUTH
NICODEMUS

Page 20 Mary Magdalen

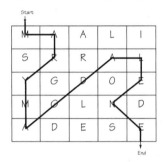

Page 21 Martha

Page 22 Lazarus

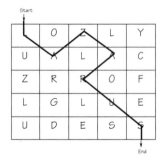

Page 23 Prodigal Son

Page 24 Mary

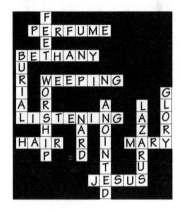

Page 25 Pilate
1. crucifixion
2. innocence
3. Barabbas
4. governor
5. prisoner
6. Praetorium
7. Golgotha
8. executed
9. Pilate

Page 26 Thomas

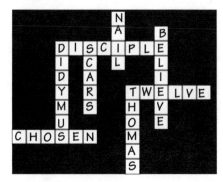

Page 27 Sapphira
1. APOSTLES
2. PETER
3. SATAN
4. HOLY SPIRIT
5. DIED
6. HOURS

Page 28 Peter

Page 29 Paul
1. Corinth
2. Galatia
3. Colosse
4. Philippi
5. Ephesus

Page 30 Barnabas